HASTA BRATA
Classic Javanese Symbolic, Philosophical, and Ethical
Leadership Teaching

AHMAD DZIKRAN

(@ahmaddzikran)

Opening Words

The Java Island of Indonesia has cultural values and philosophy that are adopted to guide the moral, social, economic, and political aspects of its residents' life.

As a tradition and culture, the Javanese civilization is very rich with moral ethics and a guide system for leaders/kings that were written in several manuscripts.

One of the leadership books in ancient Java is *Hasta Brata* from Sanskrit, which means Eight (*Hasta*) Attitudes (*Brata*), as a code of conduct for a king to lead the people fairly.

As a legacy of feudalistic tradition, Hasta Brata did not give kings any space to impose authoritarian policies, because they were tied to the moral values in the guide system. *Hasta Brata* called kings and people to jointly create harmonious relationships and strengthen the country by achieving national welfare.

Undoubtedly, *Hasta Brata* is still relevant to be applied as leadership guidance in modern times. Every leader or manager should read and learn *Hasta Brata*.

Table of Content

KEJAWEN (JAVANISM) AS A LIFE PRINCIPLE ON JAVA ISLAND

Since 3000 years BC, the ancient people of Java had known wet-rice cultivation. This system of agriculture requires smooth cooperation between villagers and is still being practiced to this day. The villagers must have very high awareness to organize such a complicated arrangement so they can have good cooperation that benefits all parties involved. Other than wet-rice cultivation, they have also known for their fishery, astronomy, cloth weaving, batik, gamelan, and wayang, among others. Before the arrival of Hinduism and other world religions, the Javanese people already had a culture and belief(s) of their own.

In some Javanese traditional ceremonies, ancient rituals remain in place to this day. It is proof that Javanese people care deeply about preserving their precious identity. Besides the existence of widely recognized religions such as Hinduism, Buddhism, Islam, and Christianity, a local belief popularly known as **Kejawen** or **Kebatinan** (spiritualism) does continue to exist.

Kejawen (Javanism), from the word Jawa (Java), is a Javanese spiritual knowledge in search of a good and correct way of life. Therefore, the person who practices its teachings correctly and wholeheartedly should find the spiritual way to true life (**urip sejati** => *urip* = life, sejati = true) and achieve the harmonious relation between servant and God, or in Javanese ***Jumbuhing Kawulo Gusti*** (*jumbuh* = a good, harmonious relation; *kawula* = servant; *gusti* = Lord, God).

This is **Kasunyatan** - The Reality, **Kebatinan** from the word *Batin* = inner, spiritual. *Kebatinan* (spiritualism) is generally understood as the spiritual teaching of belief in one God.

Some opinions say that *Kejawen* has a broader meaning than *Kebatinan*, except that *Kebatinan* also consists of the way of thinking, art, tradition, culture, etc.

The existence of *Kejawen* in no way can be separated from the Javanese way of life and thinking and its nature and tradition.

A Javanese concept that still prevails to this day is **Mamayu Hayuning Bawono,** which means to preserve the beauty of the world in a broader sense, which then translates into preserving the universe for the welfare of its inhabitants.

By nature, a Javanese is an environmentalist or a preserver of nature as clearly shown in their natural tradition and ritual orientation.

To the Javanese people, living in harmony is important, which refers to the harmonious relationship among people in society, between human beings and the universe, and between servants and God.

Since their tender ages, the Javanese had been educated by their parents, families, society, teachers, etc, the lessons of belief in God, moral behavior, and etiquette.

The Javanese elderly always said **that all**

religions are good. Until today there is barely any conflict in Java because of religious differences.

Up to the present date, the four royal palaces in Yogyakarta and Surakarta (*Kasultanan* under Sultan Hamengku Buwono X, *Pakualaman* under Viceroy/ Adipati Pakualam IX, *Kasunanan* under Sunan Paku Buwono XII, *Mangkunagaran* under Adipati/ Viceroy Mangkunagara IX) have become the centers of Javanese court culture, where royal ceremonies from the old days are still performed.

INTRODUCTION TO JAVANESE MORAL BEHAVIOR, ETIQUETTE, AND TRADITION

As a society that has existed since ancient times, Javanese people have traditional values that guide them to do the right things. Among these traditional values are :

BUDI PEKERTI

Meaning Good conduct of life/good morality. This is the most important moral guidance for traditional Javanese.

Someone who possesses *budi pekerti* is supposed to live in safety (*slamet*) and never be in trouble.

Parents' or elder people's blessings always start with the word "*Slamet*". *Budi Pekerti* is the mother of all other ethics, good behavior, proper conduct, etc.

The stories of *wayang* (shadow puppet performance) are some of the most important sources of *Budi Pekerti's* lessons for youngsters. There are even episodes in wayang that show the way to reach the true life (*urip sejati*) or the unity of servant and Lord (**Manunggaling Kawulo Gusti**: *manunggal* = unity; *kawulo* =servant; *Gusti* = Lord).

In the episodes of *wayang*, the Javanese see their own life. Through a *wayang* show, Javanese are being taught, insinuated, criticized, and reminded about their own behavior. That is why *wayang* is very popular in Java until now.

The lessons from *Wayang* include:

1. There are good and evil, and in the end, the good shall win. But anytime, evil will try to keep tempting us.

2. Follow the examples of *Pandawas* and other *Satrias* (Knights, Warriors with noble character), who are known for their noble character, sincerity, and politeness. They fight for the truth, for the welfare of the people and the country. They learn spiritualism earnestly and use their supernatural power to accomplish a noble goal.

3. Do not follow the deeds of *Kurawas* and their cronies. They are never sincere, always greedy for power and material wealth, and rude. They look only to fulfill their lust. In Javanese *wayang*, the cronies of Kurawas are often depicted in the form of *Buto*, a giant

troll, which also means 'blind' (a person who sees no difference between good and bad).

4. The dwellers of the universe are not only human beings and animals. There are also other creatures such as spirits (bad and good ones) or popularly known as "*mahluk alus*" or unseen creatures (*mahluk* = creatures, *alus*= unseen). The Gods and Goddesses are living in their domain of *Kahyangan* (the abode of Gods). The power holder of the universe is the Supreme God.

5. A person's life, place, and fate are pre-destined by the supernatural power of God.

6. A human being is obliged to be grateful to God as he/she has been allowed to live on earth and worship Him. One should not complain to Him when suffering, instead she/he should surrender to Him.

The legends of Java give some examples of:

1. Just and unjust Kings/Rulers

2. Deceit and Sincerity

3. Heroes and Traitors

4. Prosperous and peaceful country and chaotic country

5. (Political) Power for the people and abuse of power

6. The society of *adil* (just), *makmur* (prosperous), *Tata Tentrem Kerta Raharja* where order, peace, safety, and happiness are well maintained to create an ideal society for the Javanese.

From parents and families, teachers and society, a Javanese shall learn, among other things:

MANNERS (*tata krama*)

Manners (*tata krama*) or etiquette involves body language and gestures, such as how to sit or speak. With elder people and people of higher rank, a *krama inggil* (refined language) is used. Among friends, usually, a *ngoko* (low-level) language is spoken. Almost all words in Krama and Ngoko languages are different.

The Javanese language is unique in terms of how it functions to show the *tata krama* (etiquette).

RESPECT

A Javanese should respect parents, elder people, teachers, and ancestors. It does not mean that younger people should not be respected – they should be treated with the same regard, too. The same courtesy should also be shown to persons with higher and lower positions.

This *Tata Susila* (ethics) also includes:

- To be honest, not to cheat, ready to help others.

To well behave by avoiding **mo limo** (5 bad conducts in the Javanese language starting with **mo**); **Main** - gambling; **Madon** - committing adultery; **Mabuk** - excessive alcoholic drinking; **Madat** - using opium, narcotics, etc; **Maling** - stealing. Needless to say, killing and cruelty must be avoided too.

- To have proper behavior and avoid wrongdoings to protect a good reputation, so that one should not feel **isin** (ashamed). To feel "*isin*" due to bad conduct for a Javanese is shameful and makes one feel like losing their honor.

- To maintain harmony (**rukun**) and not to spark conflicts in the family, the neighborhood, the village, the country, and the world. The harmonious relationship between men is important. Factually any destruction in life is almost always caused by irresponsible human beings. Only a very small part is caused by animals and/or spirits. A popular proverb says:

  Rukun agawe santoso, which means harmony makes us strong.

- To be patient (**sabar**), or to have self-control.

- To accept fate sincerely and not to envy others' success (**nrimo**)

- To not be selfish or act only for our interest. Or in Javanese, *sepi ing pamrih* (free of self-interest). ***Sepi ing pamrih, rame' ing gawe*** in a broader sense means free of self-interest, and always ready to work hard for the interest of the society and the welfare of the world. *Rame* (crowded, hype) refers to the description of being active. The antonym of *rame* is *sepi* (quiet), which is an illustration of not hoping for any rewards (*pamrih*). *Gawe* itself means 'works'.

SLAMETAN

Slametan is a very important tradition. It is a religious ritual attended by neighbors and/or relatives and/or some close friends. They usually gather to have a simple ceremonial feast where there are offerings of rice cones (*tumpeng*), some side dishes, fruits, betel leaves, petals of flowers, etc.

Slametan derives from the Javanese word "*slamet*" (safe) and is intended as a kind of prayer for safety, including in work, birth, marriage, death, and so forth.

GOTONG ROYONG

This phrase means 'communal work', or the act of consciously and deliberately helping each other, especially in the neighborhood or in the village, for example in *bersih desa* (village cleansing), repairing the neighborhood roads, guarding the safety of the neighborhood or the village, or voluntarily helping a neighbor's funeral.

THE LEVELS OF KEJAWEN (JAVANISM)

There are 3 levels of kejawen knowledge:

1. Level 1: It is called **Kanuragan**, from the word "*Raga*", which literally means 'body.' This term refers to the various styles found in the traditional Javanese art of self-defense. The body of a *Kanuragan* student usually gains strength and invulnerability (against bullets, sharp weapons, etc.). *Kanuragan* is popular among youngsters. Followers of this discipline usually believe more in mystical or supernatural power.

2. Level 2: It is called **Kasepuhan**, from the word "*Sepuh*", which means 'old.' This knowledge is mainly used to cure sick people, physically and/or mentally. It gives protection to those who are looking for *slamet* (safety in life, well-being, etc.)

3. Level 3: It is called **Ngelmu Sejati** (true knowledge) or **Kasunyatan** (True Reality). A good and wise person, who has successfully achieved true knowledge, sees the true Reality of life. All are open for him/her and there are no more secrets in life.

A true Javanese person would not feel satisfied before he could achieve the True Reality, which refers to harmonious relations between servant and Lord (*Jumbuhing Kawulo Gusti*). One might be good in *Kasepuhan*, but if he/she still feels worried, then she/he would not gain inner peace. This often leads them to visit their ancestors' graves where they would ask for help or go to dukun (*shaman*) to ask for solutions to their problems.

To master the True Reality, it takes a long and devout exercise and practice of using self-inner energy. Only a mature, honest, wise person is able to gain this true knowledge, as he/she would need divine permission.

Note:

In addressing people, the Javanese use expressions they usually use among family members. Elder men or respected men are addressed as **Pak**, the short form of **Bapak** (father), or Mr in English. In high-level language (Kromo), it is **Romo**. Elder women or respected women are addressed as **Bu**, the short form of **Ibu** (mother), or Mrs / Madame in English.

To address much older men, **Mbah**, the short form of **Simbah** (grandma or grandpa) is used. Or in Kromo (high-level) language, it is **Eyang: Eyang Kakung** (grandpa), and **Eyang Putri** (grandma). **Mas,** the short form of *Kamas* (elder men), is used for men of the same age, elder or younger. Younger men are also addressed as **Dimas**. In the common Javanese language, *Kang (Kakang)* is used instead of kamas, and *Dik* or *Di (adik/adi)* instead of *Dimas*.

As for elder women or respected women, **Mbak (Mbakyu)** is used. For younger women, it is **Jeng (Diajeng)** which means *adik* (little sister). **Nak,** from the word *ana*k (son/daughter), is used to

11

address young people who are the same age as their children. In refined language, it is **Nak Mas** (son) or **Nak Jen** (daughter). Meanwhile, **Ki** is used to address an elder respected man, and **Nyi** for an elder respected woman.

Tri Darma

Tri (Three), *Darma* (Obligation). A man with noble character is determined to do his duty in life. **Darma is a gift from the heart, pure compassion for mankind, with no selfish traits.** In a world filled with darkness and obstacles, the darma of a noble holy person is needed to solve all difficulties and problems.

One should know that from *kebatinan* point of view, God the Almighty never punishes humans. A man only receives the consequences of his deeds. A man with noble character is aware of his duty in society - he dares to defend truth, justice, and holiness.

As long as human life, he/she should also **makarti** (to do something, physically or mentally) for the benefit of mankind, because the Creator will not change the condition of a people until they change what is in themselves. And the act should be directed to the good of life and the safety of mankind.

Life and mankind would benefit greatly if there are more people with good cipta than those with bad cipta in this world. Below are three types of darma (*Tri Darma*) as good examples.

Darmane' Pandito Utomo. The darma of a noble saint. In a *wayang* story, the leading figure, Arjuna become **Begawan Mintaraga, Cipta Ening**. *Mintaraga* means to devote his entire life to the Creator; *cipta* = to create, to make; *ening*: clear and holy. Arjuna prayed to Bhatara Guru (one of the high-rank Gods in Hinduism) for the victory of his brothers, Pandawas, in the Baratayuda war because they were on the right side. To convey his plea, Arjuna did *Cipta Ening* (meditation) in a quiet place. While doing his meditation, Arjuna had to face various temptations that would interfere with his concentration. The distraction appeared in the form of beautiful goddesses who were trying to seduce him. But Arjuna would not let them fail his meditation until his plea was granted. It was an example of the darma of a noble priest/pandito.

Darmane Ratu Binatara. The darma of a great king. King Kresna of the Dwarawati Kingdom was the incarnation of the Hindu God Wisnu. He was assigned to preserve the world. He had two powerful heirlooms, namely:

1. **The flower of Wijaya Kusuma**
   It means the essence of noble behavior, which made him wise and able to see what was going to happen.

2. **C   a   k   r   a**
   A powerful weapon to destroy the evil of the world and the evil in the heart of human beings

so that the safety of the world is guarded. Krisna was a great king who always did everything in line with proper *cipta* (to create), *rasa* (sensitive sense), and *karsa* (will). That way he was able to fulfill his *darma* perfectly. Despite his greatness, Krisna was not cruel. He protected his people and always tried to uphold justice. As a ruler he held the principles of *"sepi ing pamrih rame ing gawe"* - free of self-interest, always ready to work hard - for the society and the welfare of the world. He always kept his promise, a trait popularly known as *sabda pandita ratu*.

Darmane' Satria Wiratama. The darma of a knight/warrior. A *satria* must have a darma to defend truth, justice, and holiness. If necessary, he should sacrifice his life. In *Wayang*, Patih Suwanda or Sumantri had faithfully served his king, Arjuna Sasrabahu from the Maespati kingdom. Any seeker of true knowledge will benefit from following Tri-Darma.

From this *Darmane Ratu Binatara* principle, emerged some leadership values that were popular in traditional Javanese society, one of them being Hasta Brata.

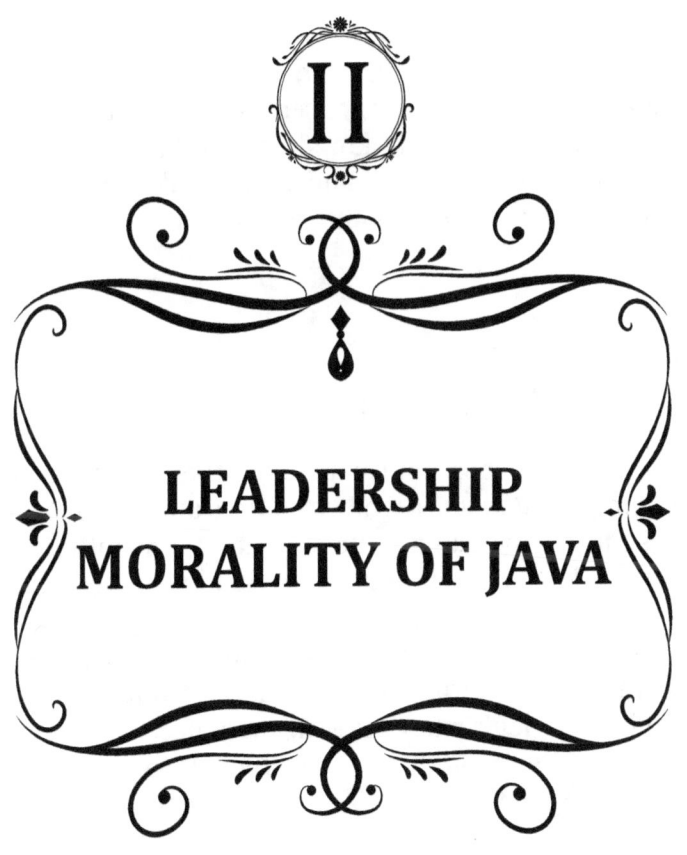

II

LEADERSHIP
MORALITY OF JAVA

L eadership in Javanese culture has deep philosophical meaning, which involves a guide and control for leaders in running the power. These values are even more effective in keeping kings or leaders from abusing their power.

From centuries ago until today, leadership morality has been practiced and still used as a reference in small kingdoms in Java like the Sultanates of Yogyakarta and Solo (Surakarta) which are considered the remainings of Javanese ancestral values.

MORAL COMMAND OF THE KING

Taking responsibility to rule the people is a command (*dhawuh*), which requires duty and moral responsibility. Ruling the people is an authority by the king's command. In the feudalistic age, the kingdom is a symbolic portrait of the valuable moral order. In terms of cultural anthropology, the palace always saw legitimacy as a moral mandate. The higher the legitimacy level in the palace, the more moral order would be embraced by the citizens. According to Geetz (1992: 145), legitimation is anthropologically a leader's effort to control other people. The authorization is then blended with the moral order.

Sri Sultan Hamengku Buwono X (2010) was the King of Yogyakarta that successfully adapted to the changing times but remained capable of maintaining the traditional moral order of Java. The Sultan always made it clear in meetings with his people that the leadership values of Java are still very relevant to be reviewed and actualized in the current global era. Of course, certain aspects should be adapted to the demands, challenges, and time of application. The leadership philosophy of Java itself can be acquired by studying the teachings of *Manunggaling Kawula Gusti* which consists of two substances: leadership and citizenship. This was particularly evident in the patriotic character of Sang Amurwabumi (Ken Arok's title) which described the synthesis of the *bhairawa-anoraga* attitude, which is 'mighty on the outside, gentle on the inside.'

The leadership of a Javanese king did have a specificity because he was the central decision-maker. This was manifested in the behavior that was always pointed and rooted to the earth, or *bhumi Sparsa mudra*. The point was the people-oriented leadership that was committed to being faithful, having steadfast, solid, and tolerant character, always doing good, and being social. In a seminar on Leadership in the Millennium III some time ago, I had the chance to explain the principles of the leadership of Sultan Agung (one of the ancient kings of Mataram Kingdom, Central Java 1613-1645), which is expressed through *Serat Sastra Gendhing* (classic Javanese literature manuscript written by Sultan Agung in the 19th century), which contains seven moral rules as a fundamental value and reminder that leadership is a noble mandate. This manuscript is the accumulation of moral teachings on the leadership of Mataram Kings. Below are seven moral values of leadership according to *Serat Sastra Gendhing* :

First, *Swadana Maharjeng-tursita.* A leader must be an intellectual figure, who is knowledgeable, honest, capable of maintaining his/her honor, and able to establish communications on the principle of independence basis. **Second,** *Bahni -bahna Amurbeng- Jurit.* A leader should be people's ultimate role model in defending justice and truth. **Third,** *Rukti-setya Garba-Rukmi.* A leader must be highly determined to gather all the power and potential for the nation's prosperity and dignity. **Fourth,** *Sripandayasih- Krani.* A leader must be committed to keeping the sacredness of religions, morals, and culture for the benefit of the community. **Fifth,** *Gaugana- Hasta.* A leader should develop literature, verbal arts, and dance to build the nation's civilization. **Sixth,** *Stiranggana-Cita.* A leader is a culture conservationist and developer, the knowledge enlightenment originator, and the bearer of the torch of happiness to mankind. **Seventh,** *Smara bhumi Adi-manggala.* A leader should be able to unify the various interests from time to time, as well as play a key role in creating the peace in *Mayapada* (mortal world). **Eighth,** *Smara bhumi Adi-manggala.* A leader should be committed to guarding the unity of various interests and play an instrumental role in establishing peace in *Mayapada*.

There is also another morality leadership doctrine, such as *Serat Wulang Jayalengkara* that says a ruler must have the character of *Wong Catur* (four terms), namely, *Retna, Estri, Curiga,* and *Paksi*. **Retna,** or gem, is a symbol of the guardian character. The nature of a precious stone is seen as something that provides peace and protection. **Estri's** (female) character is virtuous, patient, polite, and able to defeat the enemy without violence but with clever diplomacy instead. **Keris** represents a shrewd character, meaning that a leader should have sharp thinking in setting policy and strategy. The last symbol, **Paksi** (birds), represents independence. Birds are free to fly anywhere. Their freedom symbolizes the ability to act independently and not be bound to any fraction of interests in the community. This way a leader's decisions can be accepted by all levels of society.

The above examples show how rich the teachings of our ancestors are. Not to mention the very illustrious teachings contained in *Hasta Brata* or other leadership philosophies such as those represented by the *Five Pandawas* with their clown servants, the loyal and sincere Semar, and his three children. The possible elaboration and application of these teachings in modern leadership have invited humanists and scholars alike to study them.

Meanwhile, to understand our existence, it may be useful to turn the chronicle pages of *Giyanti*, when Prince Mangkubumi, who was later known as the reigning Sultan Hamengku Buwono I, launched a guerrilla war against the Dutch colonialists in Kedu and Kebanaran region, Central Java. As quoted in the Giyanti Chronicle, Mangkubumi once humbly said, *"Satuhune Sri Narapati Mangunahnya Brangti Wijayanti"* (indeed the nobles were hit with strong love).

This remark shows his concern that Western culture as a result of strangling Dutch colonialism would undoubtedly make the kings of Java plagued with romance fever and weaken them because they had chosen to join hands with the colonialist, instead of fight them. They were afraid of losing their position as kings or nobles. This situation should be faced with *wijayanti* (love, sincerity, and pure heart) to be victorious and achieve freedom. So, Mangkubumi suggested *puwarane sung awerdi, gagat-gagat – wiyati,* which means to be a winner, a king should emulate sincerity without expecting anything in return, to welcome the bright future as *Nirmala* (holy, undefiled).

This feels very relevant to the present situation, that when we are facing the swift currents of globalization, we should not just sit around, but prepare to improve our quality in all aspects of life. We should be *Eling lan Waspada* (Aware and Alert) in facing the temptations and trials in this era of *Kalatidha* (madness), where a lot of things are covered by *tidha-tidha* (full of anxiety, doubts, and uncertainty.)

Some kings who chose to remain silent against the colonialists on one hand helped reinforce the Dutch colonialism in Indonesia, particularly in Java. As a result, they lost the respect and trust of people. In this clash, Javanese cultural values became more difficult to grasp, particularly the immaterial

20

aspects such as *kawruh jiwa* (power of the soul), which was supposed to be the mental foundation of Javanese kings in facing difficult situations, including colonialism.

According to several ancient manuscripts of Java such as *Serat Niti Raja Sasana*, it is said that to maintain authority in the eyes of people, every government must uphold the principle of *"Satyawacana"* or ***"leader must carry out what he says"***. As seen today, too many promises are made instead of actual actions. We hear more about symbolic expression than information transparency. This is because today many of us, both the ruler and the people are always looking for symbols instead of meanings in almost every event.

At certain times, symbols are required, but when they are overused, they lose their meanings. Actual actions are no longer appreciated. Instead, we worship symbols and forget the essence. This has become a great concern, especially when leaders are supposed to be role models in society.

Some examples of symbolic statements expressed by leaders are: "The president expressed deep condolences over the tragedy in Ukraine", or "The president strongly condemns violence against women". These statements will only become verbal symbols if the leaders do not do any follow-ups to the problems. In other words, leaders who count on verbal symbols do not possess a *Styawacana* principle.

In line with a dialectical process, where there is

always a shift in the values of times, what is revealed in the later period is the emergence of new syntheses of leadership concepts in a state system setting that is very different from the Mataram period in the past.

Here we can conclude that we should be able to adopt the Javanese leadership through different times without having to abandon the Javanese traditional principles. A qualified Java leader is able to maintain the symbolic or spiritual meanings and then translate them into actual policy.

MORALITY AS MEASUREMENT IN JAVANESE LEADERSHIP

Moral values are the foundation of leadership philosophy in Java. A leader's quality can be measured by their morality. If a leader does sexual harassment or has an affair with other women/men, then their morality should be questioned. This also applies to leaders who abuse their power.

A leader's morale is reflected through his/her behavior. It's the compass that guides their actions. A leader with good morals will always mind his/her actions. Conversely, a lack of morals will lead to unscrupulous actions. Thus, if a Javanese leader takes the state's money illegally or does money laundering, he/she commits an act of corruption, which indicates low morale.

Each leader has an ideology that includes a set of moral values. This ideology becomes the foundation of every policy that the leader makes. In Java, an ideology is always associated with *kejawen* (javanism). The Javanese people are usually concerned with violent actions in individual life, therefore they prefer gentle leadership to be applied to the community. A gentle leader is usually a highly moral person, but this kind of leader usually attracts great enemies.

What is meant by enemy here is not an individual or a community. The main enemies of a leader with the *Satyawacana* principle and good morals are mainly individuals or groups within his territory that are obsessed with individualism, sectarianism, excessive liberalism, and a false understanding of human rights. People who think fractionally are only concerned about their perspective and act without any regard for ethics, norms, morality, and law.

Power and leadership are two interrelated things. Power is a secular result of political events that happen as relations between humans. Morally, political power should not be arbitrary, because power requires ethical leadership: wise, empathic, and just. A good leader has to have a moral guide to control his power so it would not oppress his people.

These moral values will determine whether or not a leader can survive in complex and corrupt situations. Such situations would be a tough challenge for a leader with low morality, as morality is the reflection of the soul. If his moral is good he will

23

keep his promise as a leader, by upholding justice and not abusing his power. In other words, morality is a very important trait that must be possessed by a leader if he wants his position to last.

MORALITY AND STRONG INTUITION IN JAVANESE LEADERSHIP

As a concept that contains abstract values, leaders in Java are trained and taught to sharpen their intuition. A sharp intuition is the ability to sense the abstract, unseen, or hidden things which is needed by a leader to run the country. An intuitive leader would be able to understand the people's aspirations whether they express them or not, and he can give accurate predictions on certain matters.

This strong intuition is also called *raos gesang* or feeling of life, an esoteric knowledge that every traditional king in Java should learn. A leader who has mastered *raos gesang* will attempt to change any negative circumstances because his intuition would never approve of any condition or situation that is against his leadership principle. In this phase, *raos gesang* has created a confident, firm, and determined leader who always shows affection to his people, especially the poor.

Raos gesang is derived into three characters, i.e. (1) *Bisa rumangsa*, which means a leader should keep his intuition in balance and stable. Raos gesang can indeed bring out a confident leader, but overconfidence can lead to arrogance. If a leader can manage this intuition, he will stay down to earth. (2) *Angrasa wani*, which means a brave leader should take a risk for his people. Passive leaders are usually unable to make a breakthrough. They rarely make quick decisions, and when they do, the decisions often have no clear direction. (3) *Angrasa kleru lan bener tur pener,* which means a good leader is ready to confess when he makes mistakes, and never hesitates to apologize to his people. Likewise, a good leader knows whether or not he does the right things.

Intuition helps guide the soul of leadership. Strong intuition and a gentle heart would not make a hot-headed leader. Intuition is instrumental for a Javanese leader to decide because feeling, in addition to mind, is the soul of Javanese culture.

THE SIGNS OF MORAL POWER

Thus, the Javanese tradition of political thinking typically emphasizes the previews of power concentration, not acts that show its usage. These signs are sought by good people within the power-holders as well as the societies in which they hold power. These two aspects are indeed related to each other. In other words, "a central concept of traditional Javanese view of life is a direct link between a person's state of mind and their ability to control their environment."

In a remarkably consistent way, the clearest sign of a person who has power is their ability to concentrate. This includes focusing on their power, absorbing power from the outside, and bringing together all the aspects that seem contradictory within themselves. One usual aspect of the Javanese writing tradition is the stories of historic kings as gods incarnate that we can find in *Wayang Kulit* (traditional Javanese leather puppet). One of the *wayang* characters associated with this absorption type is shown in a fight between a warrior with a strong enemy: after the enemy was defeated, his soul then enters the warrior's body and increases his strength.

A famous example is the story of King Parta who entered Arjuna's body (one of Pandawas) after he lost the battle. Another story in *Wayang* depicts the spirit of Begawan Bagaspati descending upon Yudhisthira to enable him to kill Prabu Salya or the unification of Srikandi and Ambalika to deal with the collapse of Resi Bisma. This reveals the parallel patterns where power is absorbed from the external source.

This means a leader must be able to concentrate all sources of power both from the inside and the outside to achieve his objective. If the objective is people's prosperity, a leader can utilize internal sources (domestic) and external (foreign) to achieve it.

A king can not achieve prosperity without establishing order and peace in society. These two main elements, prosperity, and order, are expressed

26

in a very old Javanese motto: *Tata Tentrem Kerta Raharja* (orderliness, peace, prosperity, and happiness). Prosperity and orderliness are part of a ruler's mission. In addition to maintaining discipline and punishment, power should also function to create a prosperous life.

When Europe found a new leadership concept, the Javanese had already applied its principles. This sense of leadership is aligned with the leadership philosophy that came from Europe. When Europeans discuss basic leadership principles such as *The Leadership Trilogy (sense of belonging, sense of participating voluntarily defend, sense of introspection)*, these values have existed and were taught in Java during the era of King Mangkunegara I (died 1795) by the name *Tri Brata* (*Tri=* Three, *Brata* = Attitude).

This Javanese *Tri Brata* consists of three attitudes: *rumangsa melu handarbeni, wajib melu hangrukebi, mulat sariro hangrasa wani.*

Rumangsa melu handarbeni means having a sense of belonging. People should love their country and therefore they will have a sense of belonging, including to the political institutions that exist. The sense of belonging to the country that we love will inspire us to contribute to a political life constructively by providing advice, feedback, and criticism.

Mulat sarira hangrasa wani is a *sense of introspection* that would help us make new decisions. One should look inside the heart and ask honestly whether his/her speech and deeds are in harmony or not. This kind of sense gives us confidence before we do something and keeps us on the right values. A leader with *mulat sarira* will have a humble and caring character.

Meanwhile, *Wajib Melu Hangrukebi* means that everyone must defend their country. That the country belongs to each citizen means it is their responsibility to defend it until the last blood.

Thus, this sense of belonging will underpin every leader's decisions and make him a respected character. A leader who runs the power based on this principle will be a dignified figure. He is fully aware that any leader could make mistakes. Leaders who possess this Javanese sensitivity are expected to be more successful, as they will be unselfish and wiser.

III

HASTA BRATA - 8 CHARACTERISTIC OF EXCELLENT LEADERS

According to the stories of *Wayang*, when King Rama passed away, there was a rumor spreading in the whole country that his eight-jeweled crown called *Makuta Rama* had lost. This rumor made everyone busy trying to find the crown, including Arjuna. Desperate that his quest was fruitless, Arjuna asked his master to give him *wangsit* (*divine inspiration*) about where he could find *Makuta Rama.* The master laughed loudly and then told Arjuna that *Makuta Rama* was merely a symbol. Those eight jewels were the *Hasta Brata,* (*Hasta* = eight, *Brata* = attitude), the eight types of attitudes that should guide a leader to run the country.

To Javanese, the term *Hasta Brata is* very familiar. The concept of *Hasta Brata* itself is well known, not only in Java but also throughout Indonesia. It's a concept of kindness teachings that should be understood and practiced by every human living in this world, especially leaders.

In *wayang* stories, the vast teachings of *Hasta Brata* had successfully led two great Kingdoms to glorious ages. These two Kingdoms were ruled by the royal reincarnation of Bathara Wisnu (one of the Prime Gods in Hinduism), who was Sri Rama Wijaya (King of Ayodya, mentioned in epos of *Ramayana*) and Sri Bathara Kresna (King of Dwarawati, mentioned in *Mahabharata*).

This concept of *Hasta Brata* was not just an ordinary kind of knowledge - it was called *Ilmu Pethingan, a* high-level knowledge that only those with sincere hearts would be able to understand it. Without a sincere heart and strong will, this knowledge would be impossible to learn.

Furthermore, *Hasta Brata* is supposed to be the guide of living for any Javanese - it should be absorbed into our hearts and practiced in our daily life. In other words, *Hasta Brata* is a set of characters a good man should have to improve his personality and soul in this life.

As previously mentioned, *Hasta Brata* teaches us to follow the examples of nature's elements in life. Those eight elements of nature that become the symbols of noble characters are (1) Earth Character (*laku hambeging kisma*); (2) Water Character (*laku hambeging tirta*); (3) Wind Character (*laku hambeging maruka*); (4) Ocean Character (*laku hambeging baruna*); (5) Moon Character (*laku hambeging candra*); (6) Sun Character (*laku hambeging surya*); (7) Fire Character (*laku hambeging dahana*); (8) Star Character (*laku hambeging kartika*).

1. LEADER WITH EARTH CHARACTER (*LAKU HAMBEGING KISMA*)

A leader should have the character of the earth. Since ancient times, the earth had become humans' foothold for its strength and safety. Though a lot has been done to the earth, still it never stops showing its generosity, growing everything for any creatures living on it. All kinds of plants grow on Earth. It even conceals treasures such as gold for us to find.

A leader with earth character should have positive behavior: *"Sepi Ing Pamrih. Rame Ing Gawe,"* always works hard and never expects anything in return. In short, he/she is dependable. A leader must strive to provide what the people need without any conditions. Unfortunately, in this modern day, a lot of political leaders demand the people do something beneficial for them so they can reach the top position. But once he gets what he wants, this leader abandoned the people who helped him in the first place. This is why a lot of people see politics as nothing more than business. You can not take anything without giving first. You sell and you buy.

A leader should show affection to all of his people, in the way that Earth loves every creature stepping on it by growing everything they need. Earth always finds a way to heal itself no matter what humans do to it. Earth does not care. It just wants to present happiness and prosperity to the living creatures.

Earth, with its ability to grow living things, is a symbol of a leader who educates his people to become qualified individuals. He does not only lead them, but he also educates, trains, and helps create the best generation, from whom a good leader is born for the future.

A leader should not focus on how to maintain his power, but he should think about the country's sovereignty and the prosperity of the people. This would include preparing potential leaders for the future to continue his people-oriented policies.

Another characteristic of the Earth is its ability to remove ugliness. When a human dies, the Earth absorbs the flesh and leaves only the bones. Similarly, a leader should be able to eliminate the bad sides of his people such as laziness, corruption, lack of discipline or education, crimes, etc. More importantly, a leader should get rid of his negative character which potentially threatens his leadership.

This leads to the big mission of being a leader: changing the people for the better, by providing better education, changing conflicts into harmony, and inspiring an individualistic community into one that is full of solidarity.

2. LEADER WITH WATER CHARACTER (*LAKU HAMBEGING TIRTA*)

Water always flows to find the lower surface, and when it flows, water is filling every part in the way it passes through. Similarly, a leader should be able to place himself among his people to find out what problems they are having. He should not be attached to the elite or upper class of society. Instead, he should put his people's (especially the poor) interests above anything.

Water (*Tirta*) always has a flat level, meaning that a leader must treat his people fairly. He should never give privileges to anyone, be it a noble family or a wealthy or high-ranked politician. There should be no special treatment. Everything must be done properly because any kind of discrimination will ruin social life.

Justice should be upheld and spread all over the community. A comprehensive justice gives brightness to the community, in the same way that water cleans impurities. This message is presented in the saying that water never *embat oyot emban cindhe* (gives special treatment to somebody/social group).

Water gives us coolness as well. A leader with a water character will provide peace, comfort, and safety to the people because he fulfills their rights. Nobody feels hungry, no body feels unsafe, and no body feels marginalized.

This water (tirta) character is similar to the character of Yama, one of Hindu Gods who is featured regularly in *wayang kulit* shows. Yama's leadership is considered as a role model for any leaders. In the stories, he upholds justice and enforces the law no matter what it costs to guard his people. Besides *Tirta's* character, Yama also possesses what is described as a 'cloud' character, meaning that he can collect all useless or negative things around him and turn them into something valuable. Just like the pre-rain process, the vapors do not have a real purpose because they are only moving in the air, but they change into something useful for human life after they gather as overcast and then drop as rains to help make the land fertile.

So, a leader should be able to empower the people, helping them become better individuals. However, just like the lightning through the rain, he will punish anyone who breaks the rule. The flash in the rain acts as an inspector to detect something good or bad - he gives rewards to the good one and punishment to the bad one. In modern leadership theory, it is similar to what we know as the "stick and carrot rule".

Another characteristic of water is its flexibility that it shows when we fill it into the container. The same thing is expected from a leader – he should have flexibility and wisdom in managing his authority in efforts to build a better community. He does not approach people with power, punishment, or threats; instead, he motivates and inspires them to be engaged with his vision.

3. LEADER WITH WIND CHARACTER (*LAKU HAMBEGING MARUTA*)

Like the wind, a leader should be there anytime for his people and give them a breath of fresh air to their problems. The wind never stops seeing people, it always visits us. We can not see it, but we can feel its breeze. Similarly, a leader should always strive to give solutions to his people's problems, with or without media coverage, because that is what he is elected for in the first place.

Just like water, wind brushes every place when it blows. No single place is free from the wind, even the smallest corner can't deny it. A leader must have careful thinking. He should listen to every problem, and consider every possible solution before he chooses the best option.

A thoughtful leader is not necessarily a slow decision-maker. He just has to be careful not to make the wrong decision because there will always be political lobbyists with inaccurate information who are eager to use him for their interest.

Once again, we can not see the wind, but we do feel its presence when it blows. A leader with a wind character doesn't need publicity to finish his job. He should not worry about being a media darling, as more often than not, that type of publicity is created by politicians and mass media to conceal his incapability from the public's eyes. *The truth is not always what we see in the media.*

A leader with a wind character has the *Maruta* principle, which is working sincerely without media hoopla. Indeed, media coverage is important, especially when he has to make important announcements, but when it comes to the execution of his programs, too much media will affect his work.

An effective leader should just do his job mainly for the best interest of his people.

4. LEADER WITH OCEAN CHARACTER (*LAKU HAMBEGING BARUNA*)

Ocean is the largest part of the Earth – it is vast and deep. When we think about sailing the ocean, it is as if we can see the end of it, but factually, once we reach what we thought was the border, we are faced with another wider range of oceans. This endless view makes the oceans seem borderless.

A leader with an ocean character has deep insight and knowledge with which he is expected to be able to solve every problem appropriately and wisely. Our ancestors said:

"*Dadi pemimpin kang wicaksana, ora mung cukup pinter, sebab pinter tanpa wicaksana wekasane malah minteri.*"

The translation is:

"*Be a wise leader, not only smart. Because smartness with no wisdom is only charming falsehood.*"

Smartness only comes from intelligence that is created by the brain. But a wise person uses his heart in addition to his brain, which in turn manifests into morality. A leader with an ocean character has a sensitive heart. He can feel more than most people. He can identify people's problems whether or not they express them.

There are many smart leaders on this planet, leaders who graduate from prominent universities around the world with academic honors. But such achievement is not always synonymous with wisdom. They tend to count on their logical thinking and usually underestimate their sense or intuition when dealing with problems. They believe they could end most of the world's problems with their intelligence and rationale, but they fail to use their hearts to feel why such problems always exist.

In *Hasta Brata* symbolization, the ocean (and water generally) has a forgiving nature. If someone scoops up the water, it soon recovers itself completely without leaving any holes or dents. This is why in Javanese philosophy a leader must have a big and forgiving heart because he is the center of attention. It is very likely that somebody or a social group feels disappointed and expresses it bluntly.

A leader can not escape criticism from his people, and this is why he should be ready to forgive. If he reacts negatively to every criticism, it could turn him into a totalitarian leader.

A wise leader has to accommodate everything, even the things that he does not like, the same way the ocean always accepts anything that flows from the rivers, be it garbage, corpses, or waste.

The soul of the ocean reflects the ability to accept and embrace plurality in the community. The ocean knows that plurality is natural, which if denied, would result in terrible consequences because nothing can stop nature's way. If it is stuck, then imbalance and disharmony will emerge in this life.

In modern management, we know three criteria of an ideal leader, namely insight or knowledge, excellent capability, and honorable attitude or morality. A leader with these three criteria will bring the unity of *cipta, rasa,* and *karsa,* i.e. capability to create (*cipta*) or to change something (improving capability), intuition (*rasa*), and dedication (*karsa*).

So, are we leaders with an ocean character or not? We should take a moment to contemplate that.

5. Leader With Moon Character (*Laku Hambeging Candra*)

Moon (*Candra*) presents a beautiful view most nights, especially when it's full. Moon's shine is soft, it offers beauty, and the light reaches everyone. Though beautiful, the moon does not radiate heat. This implies that a leader should rule the people wisely.

We love to see the full moon at night. In the same way, we are proud of a leader for his positive influence, not because of his physical appearance or his luxurious suits. His character and wisdom succeed in making a better change in his people's life. This is how a real leader earns the people's respect.

As the moon illuminates the darkness, a leader should also be a light to his people. When everyone feels disoriented, he is expected to be visionary.

That way he can play the role of a torch for others.

With its soft light that radiates beauty around the world, the moon represents an enchanting sensibility. The same thing is expected from a leader. He should give soft light like the moon (*Purnama Sidi*) - he establishes his power with sensitivity, affection, and wisdom.

As the moon gives its light freely, a leader has to be able to provide enlightenment to his people in times of trouble and ignorance through generous empathy. Towards the unfortunate people, he should not judge or humiliate them, but be fair and affectionate.

Sociologically, we need to remember that Indonesians are generally holding a "Patron and Client" basis. A leader is a patron to the people, which means the leader is a father figure or someone to emulate. This patron-client relationship is similar to the parent-kid relationship. A child will follow and imitate his/her parent's behavior because they are their role model. So naturally, a model should give a positive example as guidance to his/her followers.

If the patron does bad or negative things, how can one expect the clients to be good? In this type of culture, a prominent figure is considered very important to be a leader (patron) in Indonesia. A Javanese proverb says, "*Agama Ageming Aji,*" which means that "the King's religion is the people's as well." The people will immediately follow what the king believes, including his religion.

A good leader should do good things truly from his heart, not for the sake of having an admirable image. If he only shows benevolence during the presidential campaign, he just wants to get more votes or manipulate the people.

Doing good things with full consciousness and responsibility is something natural for a leader with the moon character. He does it because he needs it. It is part of him. If he doesn't do it, he turns into something else that he doesn't know.

This dishonest feeling may be pleasing to him for a while. But when his power ends, such a leader will fall painfully.

Doing benevolence full of responsibility means all those good things are not fake, but they come out of his consciousness. A good leader doesn't want to be falsely judged by his people. He would not be happy that people think of him as a good leader while he lies. So he does everything for a greater cause, i.e. to improve people's life.

6. LEADER WITH SUN CHARACTER (*LAKU HAMBEGING SURYA*)

A Leader with a sun (*Surya*) character always inspires and motivates the people, like how the sun would shine on the earth and provide energy to all of the creatures. The lights travel in their direction, never haste, and bring warmth to the surface that they touch. Nothing humans can do to stop the sun from radiating its lights. In the same way, when making a decision, a leader has to put his people's interests as the top priority and not let anything interfere. His policy is decided thoughtfully to make sure that it stays in the right direction, but flexibility is applied when needed. This means that a leader has the right to make adjustments to his policy when it's necessary, rather than impose the rules rigidly.

The sun is the biggest source of energy that enables every creature on Earth to grow. Similarly, a leader is in charge of training and educating his people so they can improve their quality of life.

Shiny and bright, the sun never stops glowing. The lights shine on every corner of the universe that they can reach. A leader must lead his people to enlightenment, show them the right path, and never give up in his effort to guide them. His decision is carefully made, but in implementation, he should be firm with his objective, to make people's lives better, regardless of skin color, religion, or ethnicity.

As the main source of warmth, light, and energy, there would probably be no life without the sun. Because of the sun, all creatures can have days and nights. During the day, we work, make friends, and build relationships with other people. And at night, it is time for us to rest and relax. This is what the sun teaches us, how to fill our lives with positive and constructive things and be wise with our bodies.

In the modern political system, the heads of state have a term limit. For example in Indonesia, a President can be elected only twice for two periods

(5 years each). If he possesses and learns these Hasta Brata principles, then he wouldn't waste time by abusing his power through corruption, nepotism, and collusion. But so far, since 1998, no Indonesian President applies the Hasta Brata principles.

A leader with a sun character has great discipline as well. He treats his people affectionately as long as they follow the rules. On the contrary, he never hesitates to apply the law of punishment if they break the rules, just like the heat of the sun.

A head of state should lead the country fairly without expecting any personal gains, just as the sun never expects us to pay back what it has given. Unfortunately, most of today's leaders only sell promises to get more votes.

With its heat, the sun slowly absorbs the water, allows it to become steam then turns it into rains that in turn fertilize the soil and give life to the earth. Dried lands become lush again with greens and rivers are flowing again with streams. Leaders with the sun spirit possess energy and dedication to achieve goals based on careful thinking and persistence.

Surya or sun represents a source of spirit to create and build a country so the people can live a truly good life. This meaning is in line with the role of the sun that shines on Earth to keep this planet alive.

At the time of what we call as "global era" today, tight competition has forced people to ignore these integrity principles to achieve their goals. They do not care about the process, because their only goal is only to make their dreams happen, no matter how. They could not care less if they intentionally r unintentionally sacrifice others as long as that can bring them closer to their goals.

This attitude is truly against justice values, in which the way to achieve the goals should be more important than the goals themself. Javanese ancestors had predicted this kind of attitude in a poem :

"Mengko arep ana jaman kang kinaranan jaman edan. Yen ora edan ora komanan, nanging sabegja-begjane wong kang edan, isih begja wong kang eling lan waspada."

The loose translation is:

"Later, it would come a time of madness (*jaman edan*). If you don't follow this madness, you'll get nothing. But remember, even if you benefit from your madness, the luckier ones are those who keep their feet on the ground. They are the careful and wary ones."

As cited by the intellectuals and cultural observers in Indonesia, we are in a time of madness now. What was predicted in the poem proves to be true now with the rampant corrupt leaders, a country invading another country for its resources, hunger, and diseases, killing and anger everywhere, drugs, sex, and pornography viewed as art or industry. Honesty is abandoned but manipulation becomes normal.

We need a leader with a sun character to serve as a light in this age of global madness. Hopefully, such a leader will emerge in each region to correct all problems.

7. Leader With Fire Character (*Laku Hambeging Dahana*)

Fire has noble characteristics; it stands upright but is also flexible. It can engulf anything and burn it, but on the other side, it spreads the light when it gets dark. A leader should be patient but dedicated, full of courage, and firm like a burning fire. Regarding a leader's courage, there was a proverb in Javanese Hasta Brata that said: *"Sing sapa wani ing gampang wedi marang kang ewuh, samubarang ora tumeka,"* (Those who are only courageous dealing with the ease but scared of difficulties, will never achieve the goals).

That proverb reminds us, especially leaders, that we need the courage to live our life. As we always know, life is never a flat line. Problems are inevitable. Whether you like it or not, you have to walk through them and try to solve them.

However, the burden and responsibility are even greater for a leader because he carries the people's problems and has to come up with the best solutions. He has to provide the right solutions to prevent the same problems from reappearing the in the future.

Moreover, a leader should be capable of predicting the potential problems that may emerge among his people. This is why a leader has to possess a fire character.

Leaders with fire character speak based on the principle of *"Sabda Pandhito Ratu, Tan Kena Wola-wali"*, meaning "A leader's words are words of *pandhito*'s (religious leader), he can't be *mencla-mencle* (inconsistent)". A leader should always stay true to his words. He can not say "A" and then change into "B" at will. With this kind of leader, how would he expect his people to follow him? How can we elect someone with perplexity and without any direction?

A consistent leader thinks and says carefully. His judgment should always be based on logical thinking and deep consideration, so he would not take the wrong step. A leader with a fire character upholds accountability principles, both in his words and works. The Javanese regard such leaders as having the attribute of *Berbudi Bawa Laksana*, i.e. being consistent with his words.

A leader with such integrity will rule his country in the same way that a fire gives light in the darkness. He shows the people the path to a better future. On the contrary, an inconsistent leader will put the people into disorientation and potentially bring them into the abyss of decline.

8. Leader With Star Character (*Laku Hambeging Kartika*)

Stars (*Kartika*) are a wonderful guide. A leader with a star character is a pride to his people. He is always ready to provide guidance and his followers have confidence in him. Just as how the stars never move, and always stay where they are, a leader should also act as someone to emulate, a role model, and a collective guide. And this trait can be earned only if he is consistent with his intention to guide the people.

A leader must be strong physically and mentally. He always strives to do good for others, consistent, firm against temptation, and without pretense. This attitude should become every leader's trait.

And despite his shortcomings, a leader should always possess self-confidence. Because though very small, the stars never fail to emit their lights and beautify the sky.

Nobody is perfect. Like all human beings, leaders also have feelings, fears, and dreams. What sets them apart is their capability to control their human sides and place the public's interest as a priority. He is forced to abandon his negative character so he can light up the torch and show the people the path to a better future.

*****

The *Hasta Brata* gives us cosmic consciousness that the universe contains lessons for human beings who want to reflect and research. This universe is a great school that provides the best teachings for humans.

IV

A LEADER'S DHARMA

J avanese literature is divided into three main themes, i.e (1) *darma sastra,* which contains a lofty human obligation to others, (2) *Artha sastra,* which contains the thought of power, and (3) *kama sastra,* which discusses life problems. These three books, especially *darma sastra,* often describe what and how an ideal leader should be. Meanwhile, in *Artha Sastra,* we can find *a* discussion on the political tragedy in a kingdom.

Dharma means a leader's duty. It is related to one's obligations toward others. If those obligations are done properly, it would create social-political balance in society. On the contrary, *adharma* refers to all actions which go against a human's obligation and duty. When *adharma* is left out of control, it can cause conflicts or even bloodshed.

In the *Bharatayudha* epic, a lot of stories on *dharma* and *adharma* are told, especially when Basudewa Krisna taught Arjuna the lesson of *Bhagawadgita* to awaken his spirit because Arjuna was so distraught in his effort to accomplish his duty as a knight to defend the truth.

In *Serat Panitisastra* and *Serat Slokantara* (two ancient manuscripts on politics), the relationship between a leader and his people is likened to a lion and the forest, or the fish and water; both can not be separated. They need each other; one can not be a foe to the other. In this context, the leader and the people have a symbiotic relationship. A good and effective leader who succeeds in organizing the people will receive appreciation from his people. Consequently, people will love, follow and obey him.

It is almost impossible to break their bond because their relationship is so strong, thanks to the good works of the leader. The leader protects the people, and in return, the people will fight for his leadership. When this harmony happens, a very strong country will emerge. It is not because military forces or political influence persuade other countries to march behind its back, but it is purely because of the respect and love that people have for their leader, and vice versa. Have we seen such a country today?

In *Serat Pamarayoga*, R. Ng. Ranggawarsita (a great Javanese poet born in Kasunanan Surakarta, Central Java, in 1805) said that a king who holds the administration is the representative of *Hyang Agung* (God). The king is protected by *tri loka buwana*, namely *pinandhita* (a religious figure, a symbol of spiritual protection), *bathara* (God or Gods, blessing giver), and *satriya* (knights). A Leader should have extensive knowledge and master the *kanuragan* (self-defense knowledge), *kadigjayaan* (social, economy, political, and military insight), and *kawicaksanaan* (wisdom and intelligence). The leader identity is a very heavy *dharma* (obligation) which is divided into 8 aspects, including (1) *Hanguripi,* meaning that a leader should protect the people, respect and maintain peace based on the law so the people feel confident that they can achieve a better life. (2) *Hangrungkebi,* meaning that a leader must have the courage to sacrifice his soul, mind, and wealth for the people's welfare. As a public servant, a leader has to achieve the nation's *Mukti Wibawa* (Dignity and Honor) by gathering national strength to defend the people with *Sasanti* (motto): "United we stand, Divided we fall". (3) *Hangruwat,* meaning that a leader should tackle various problems that disrupt the government by reducing poverty, helping the disabled, and providing education for the youth so that God blesses the country with peace, convenience, and solutions. (4) *Hanata (*to manage), meaning that a leader should *"Njunjung Drajating Praja"* (Maintain The Good Governance), a motto based on the concept of *"nata lan mbangun praja"* (manage and develop the country) with discipline, honesty, and loyalty for the sake of people's welfare; be a good role model (*ing ngarsa sung tuladha*), awaken their work spirit by being the pioneer (*ing madya mangun karsa*), and encourage the people to keep working hard, improve their potentials and build their lives (*tut wuri handayani*). (5) *Hamengkoni,* (provide the frame), a metaphor that means the leader should guide his people to support his vision, goals, and national programs. This way a so national unity is realized. The government should give the people freedom to try to utilize domestic potentials and establish cooperation with other countries without intervention. (6) *Hangayomi,* from Javanese word *ayom* (protection), meaning that a leader should protect the people so they feel safe, free to work and interact. A leader is obliged to protect the people to maintain national dignity. (7) *Hangurubi,* meaning that a leader should raise people's morale to achieve collective welfare. In any country, people certainly expect welfare and the government should provide them with facilities to increase their quality of life. To make this happen, the leader must love his people and build harmonious relationships with them by sticking to the *Sabda Pandhita Ratu* principle, i.e. a leader should be committed to his words. (8) *Hamemayu*, meaning that a leader should keep the peace by fostering harmony and harmonious society based on mutual trust to prevent suspicion, to improve the government system.

From those eight teachings above, we can conclude that a leader has a noble duty. They are in charge of special tasks that can not be carried out by ordinary people. When a leader can show positive character such as being protective and unselfish, then the country will be peaceful. Furthermore, the harmonious relationship between a leader and the followers is determined by how well the leader manages the people. If he is just, then his government will not be criticized. It is typical for potential leaders to give political promises that if they are elected, they will grant the people's aspirations. But if a leader breaks those promises, then he will be labeled as *Adharma*. A leader who keeps the *dharma* will have a more secure position. Many leaders of nations today are condemned by their people. This is because they forget their dharma. Such kind of leaders are likened to a snail that forgets its shell.

The dharma of a leader is always directed at the people's happiness. Dharma is bound by sacred promises spoken by someone about to run his/her candidacy, promises that should be done immediately.

FIGURES AND REQUIREMENTS TO BE A LEADER IN JAVA

When King Sri Ajpamasa (one of the ancient kings in Java) renounced his throne, he advised his son that a king should hold the doctrines of *Pancamatra,* which are (1) *Mulad,* meaning that a leader should be alert and cautious with his servants because some of them may be cheating or giving false information/advice, (2) *Amilala,* meaning that a leader should protect and serve the people, provide gifts to loyal servants and render a good service to the country, (3) *Amiluta,* meaning that a leader should earn the people's sympathy by caring about their rights and needs so they will be confident in his leadership, (4) *Miladarma,* meaning that a leader should be wise to contribute to the world's harmony (*mamayu hayuning bawana*), (5) *Parimarma,* meaning that a leader should have affection, patience, and forgiveness.

Those criteria if applied properly will make a country strong, peaceful, and safe. The leader should do five things to maintain the prosperity of the people, such as *Ilat, Ulat, Ulah, Asih lan Asuh. Ilat* (tongue) means that a leader should speak carefully; *Ulat* (face) refers to hospitality and concern for others; *Ulah* (act) means a good attitude to follow because the leader is a mirror for his people; and *Asih* (loving). In short, a good leader sincerely loves his people and followers, cares about them equally without any discrimination, and never prioritizes the interest of his group above his people's.

The history of Indonesia has recorded quite a lot of persons that meet the requirements to be a leader. Figures such as Sultan Agung, Cut Nyak Dhien, Gadjah Mada (Majapahit Governor), Ki Hadjar Dewantara, and Sukarno, are regarded among the successful national leaders. According to the book of *Dharma Dasa,* Gajah Mada was considered the person who was able to realize the intrinsic nature of Java leadership. He was able to act *Manjing Ajur-ajer*, or ready to feel people's suffering and understand their problems, and able to find the way out. Gajah Mada was capable to apply the basic nature of Javanese leadership, namely:

(1) *Samadhi* or meditation, which was also called *manembah* (worship) was his foundation of acts. Leading people while never forgetting the *Samadhi* will always make a leader remember the Creator so he won't act carelessly. It was told that Gajah Mada always did *Samadhi* every night since he was a boy and often had a divine vision from Brahma as his guidance.

(2) *Awas* (visionary), which means to be a pioneer and have insight into the future. Gajah Mada pioneered many projects to expand the kingdom's territory and always came up with bright ideas as a leader. His visionary ideas were based on *his* attitude; he knew any possible things that might happen. In other words, he combined two leadership concepts, i.e. (a) *ngerti* (knowing) and (b) *pakarti (understanding* what action should be taken).

(3) *Greget,* which means that a leader should be a motivator to his followers. He should lift their spirit

and push them to move forward, encouraging them to work harder to achieve a prosperous life. Gajah Mada could motivate his fellow friends because he had great charisma. His friends always followed him wherever he went.

(4) *Babar binuka*, meaning a leader should apply open management while leading his people. Open leadership is more respectable than vague one. A Leader should open himself to critics or advice and at the same time be fully authoritative and independent when making decisions. A leader like this has a sensitive heart, never loses temper in front of his staff but can openly create a dialogue so his staff will not be suspicious of him.

(5) *Lantip*, meaning a leader should be capable of managing state affairs and problems. This ability will earn him the respect of the staff. A leader will gain sympathy when he is smart and creative.

(6) *Sopan dan Ramah* (Polite and friendly). Just because a leader is someone who is on top of the socio-political pyramid, it does not mean that he can act arrogant and stubborn. He should always remember that he is in his position because of the participation of the people. He exists as a leader because of them. So it is reasonable that a leader should be friendly, polite, and have pleasant expressions when he talks to people. This is the leader who does not forget where he comes from - the people.

(7) *Ngelmu* (seeking knowledge). A leader should never stop learning. He has to learn not only

scientific thinking but also spiritual science.

(8) *Ngayomi*, meaning always protecting the people and applying justice to achieve national prosperity.

(9) *Wani*, meaning that a leader should be brave, responsible, and resilient when faced with problems. He dares to take risks and stand against any challenge on the front line. He is also subject to the laws, should never insult his people, and channel the people's aspirations to his superiors.

(10) *Rengkuh*, meaning a leader should have respect for the country's wise men and heroes, and practice *semadhi* (meditation) to seek divine inspiration.

If the above ten leadership characteristics are applied, this country will achieve prosperity. Even if the leader applies only five of them, people will see improvement in their life. A reliable leader should be able to meet these requirements in his attitude and policies because he understands that such leadership teachings are very important to him. However, without actual implementation, his leadership will only be in vain. Last but not least, it is also the people's responsibility to make sure that their leader implements these teachings.

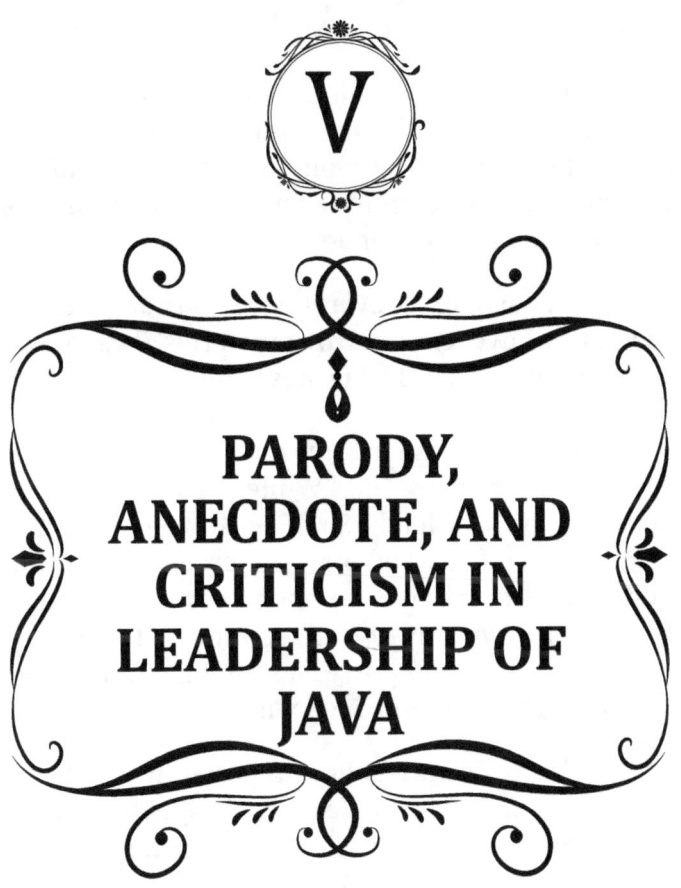

PARODY, ANECDOTE, AND CRITICISM IN LEADERSHIP OF JAVA

Parody is a funny satire to mock leaders. Through a unique character, *Dalang* (puppeteer) often tells a parodical story. The *Punakawan* group is the most appropriate character to tell the parody, where some controversy is stirred during the show.

Punakawan is a unique and famous group of characters in Wayang shows. They are the representation of common people (*Wong Cilik*), who are oppressed and very unlikely to occupy the throne and lead the kingdom.

In certain contexts, everybody is a leader. Though seen as the lower class in *Wayang* stories, *Punakawan* is a leader as well. In Javanese terminology, *Puna* means understanding, bright, clear, careful, and smart in observing the meaning behind natural events and human life. While *kawan* means a guardian or a friend. So, *Punakawan* describes someone as a friend who can observe, analyze, and understand every natural phenomenon as well as human life. *Punakawan* can also mean a caregiver or a supervisor who possesses intelligent thinking, a strong mentality, and deep wisdom.

Punakawan is the leader in a special environment, or at least for himself. As a caregiver, the words of *Punakawan* are trustworthy – there is no contradiction between what they say and what they do. In Javanese culture, Punakawan has a positive character called *tanggap ing sasmita, lan limpat pasang ing grahita,* which means "quick to understand the situation/problem, both in symbolic or real forms".

The *Punakawan* group consists of four characters: *Ki Lurah Semar Badranaya* (*Semar*), an old wise man considered as the elder of gods, and his three sons withe the name *Gareng, Petruk (means Poo Face),* and *Bagong* (*Cepot*).

Punakawan had been carrying out duties since the leadership of King Arjuna Sasrabahu from the Maespati Kingdom. Ancient Javanese Kings called *Semar* as *Kakang* (Big Brother) because his high spirituality, magical power (*sakti mandraguna*), and extensive life experiences. Even the gods called him *Kakang*.

This group of *Punakawans* was assigned to serve the *bendhara* (the bosses) who had noble attitudes. They acted as helpers and mentors at once, and their duty required them to be ready all the time. In *Wayang* stories, this group often acts more as spiritual advisors or counselors. On other occasions, they would just chat with the king and calm him down in difficult times. Many times, the *punakawans* would talk jokingly; their suggestion, ideas, and criticism are expressed in a subtle, funny, yet very meaningful way. In a certain context, *Punakawan* is the media to control the kings.

In Javanese wayang stories, Punakawans are divided into two groups; each group has the same role as spiritual and political advisors, but both of them often serve as figures with contradictory natures.

The first group is led by Ki Lurah Semar Badranaya, which consists of Semar, Gareng, Petruk, and Bagong (Cepot). They are described as honest and modest punakawan who somehow have vast knowledge and sharp inner eyes and are clever. Ki Lurah Semar, in particular, possesses a heart that is called "*nyegara*" which means 'as broad as the ocean,' and a clairvoyance as deep as the ocean as well. Only a true knight will be under Semar's nurture because Semar is a demigod whose duty is to care for the true knights.

Essentially Semar and his three sons are in charge to remind the knights to always do good things and nurture a peaceful soul (*a nafs muthmainnah*). In Islamic terminology, the phrase is probably synonymous with *amr bil ma'roof nahi 'anil munkar* (enjoining the good and forbidding the evil). They teach the knights to possess positive characters: noble, brainy, patient, sincere, alert, wise, and helpful. So, under the guidance and control of the *Punakawans,* the knights will walk on the right path. When they deviate, *Punakawans* are there to put them back on track.

The second group consists of two personnel: Ki Lurah Togog (Sarawita, Semar's brother) and Mbilung. These two *Punawakans* are responsible to accompany Ratu Sabrang (Queen Sabrang) who has a bad soul (*dur angkara*) that is filled with anger, greed, and cruelty. Besides Ratu Sabrang, Togog, and Mbilung also accompany other despotic kings: Prabu Baladewa of Mandura, Prabu Basukarna of Ngawangga, Prabu Dasamuka (Rahwana) of Ngalengka, Prabu Niwatakawaca of Iman-Imantaka and some knights from the Sabrangan land, who are huge, grumpy, silly, yet faithful to their principles. Generally, Togog and Mbilung have the task to prevent those kings and knights from *dur angkara* (inhumanity) and remind them to always be mindful, and leave all their vices and negative tendencies.

Those two groups of kings and knights project two different characters in a human soul (*jagad alit* = small cosmos). As illustrated above, the knights and kings have different and contradictory characters, meaning that in the small universe (human soul) there are two inherent natures, the good and the bad.

Other than telling about the *punakawan* tasks, some parodical stories also insinuate the king's incompetence in ruling his kingdom, such as one titled *Petruk Dadi Ratu* (Petruk Becomes a King).

As the second son of Semar, Petruk is depicted as having a nearly bare head and a long nose like Pinokio but has an honest and sincere character. Just like his two brothers, Petruk often conveys messages through humor. The presence of Petruk always gives joy because he tends to digress and entertain words. He is a servant who is attached to the aristocracy, even though he has no education or rank. In short, he is the representation of the lower class in society.

STORY OF PETRUK BECOMES A KING (PETRUK DADI RATU)

This follows the story of Jamus Kalimasada which is a very strong magical amulet in the form of a scroll owned by the Pandawas.

Dewi Mustakaweni wants to take revenge on the Pandawas after they kill one of her ancestors. She disguises herself as Gatotkaca, the son of one of the Pandawas, and easily steals Jamus Kalimasada. But before she can escape, Srikandi sees through her disguise and fights her. Dewi Mustakaweni loses and escapes. Srikandi then tells Bambang Priyambada about the stolen amulet. Bambang then chases Dewi Mustakaweni and fights her. She loses again but this time she surrenders. Bambang then gives Jamus Kalimasada to Petruk because he thought the amulet would be safe being in the hand of the highly magical Punakawan.

But instead of returning it to the Pandawas, Petruk uses the amulet for his benefit. The power of Jamus Kalimasada corrupts his mind. With the magical power of the amulet added to his magical ability, he becomes the king of Lojitenggara Sonyawibawa Kingdom, earning the title Prabu *Welgeduwelbeh Tongtongsot Upelgen Kanthong Bolong*, a funny title for a king. The title is merely a funny-sounding random name with no meaning at all, as Petruk himself is a clown character. *Kanthong Bolong* means a pocket that has a hole in it.

When Petruk becomes a king, all orders are destroyed. The knight who used his masters such as the Pandawas, King Dwarawati, and even Basudewa Krisna, now become his servants.

As a king, he is no ordinary king. His behavior as a commoner doesn't change. He still likes to eat a commoner's food and enjoys commoner's entertainment. He transforms the gardens and monuments into rice fields; knights' horses into chickens and ducks; swords and *keris* (Javanese traditional weapons) into farming tools; and temples, shrines, manors, castles, and palaces into farmhouses. Everything looks green but the distinct smell of manure is everywhere. His kingdom looks so innocent and naive, even a little stupid. Just imagine a clown becoming a king - everything is the opposite of what it used to be.

But this new state is rapidly expanding, reaching the regions of neighboring states without any bloodshed because people become citizens of this new green grassy kingdom willingly.

Seeing the new state as a threat and feeling that the new king is mocking their kingly status by ruining and changing all traditions, customs, and habits of the nobles upside down, all of the other kings become angry. Even the Gods become restless. But one by one, the knights, heroes, and gods who are sent to subdue Sonyawibawa are lost and captured. Even the king of the gods himself is lost in the battle against King Welgeduwelbeh. So, Semar, Gareng, and Bagong are sent to take a look at the situation.

Once they check out the situation in Sonyawibawa, they know that something is wrong with this kingdom and king. They recognize the problem directly before their eyes.

With his magical ability, Semar has no difficulty in entering the king's residence and appears before the king.

"Petruk, Petruk", said Semar, "Why did you do this? Don't you think that I would recognize you, my son? Are you ashamed of your status as a commoner? Do you think that a king is more noble than a commoner? Get back to your consciousness, my son, get back to yourself!"

Seeing his father, King Welgeduwelbeh immediately turns himself into the old Petruk and says:

"O, father, forgive your son. I was only curious about what it is like to be a king. Every day you get to enjoy entertainment and eat delicious food, no headache because of below standard salary, no need to strive to make ends meet and worry about being unable to pay for my son's education."

Petruk goes back to his own house and family. He hands over Jamus Kalimasada to the Pandawas, thus ending all the conflicts and problems caused by the amulet.

The story of *Petruk Dadi Ratu* describes the world imbalance, a symbol of an unqualified leader. Someone who does not qualify is elected to lead the people. It could also be interpreted as the imaginary luxuries of being a leader. During the Dutch colonial period in

Indonesia, this story arose as a veiled criticism of the Dutch colonial powers.

Well, that's the end of leadership anecdotes in the *wayang* world which is full of pretense. The point is, a leader should not only be a populist, but he should also be intellectual, spiritual, and able to feel emotions. These traits are necessary to make a national strategic policy.

Often, politicians and media create a figure they want (instead of what people want) to put that figure in the highest position in the country, regardless of his quality and capability. To them, the most important thing is they could blow up false opinions that such a figure is a suitable candidate to affect the public's choice.

Too many incapable leaders in this world are elected not because of their skill or knowledge, but merely because they are more popular in surveys and media.

Put in a modern context, the story of *Petruk Dadi Ratu* is a strong satire that mocks such leaders. They are in a top position, popular (being a media darling), but incapable.

VI

FROM JAVA TO
THE WORLD

The life of Javanese contains universal values. This universality of ethics can be traced from various philosophy of life that is closely held and maintained in Javanese daily life. This is in contrast to the understanding of many people that say that Javanese ethics are only related to manners among human beings and physical behavior. Javanese ethics put more emphasis on the "ethics of understanding" in the sense that ethics are seen as a cognitive control of some elements. In Javanese tradition, ethics is often understood as *ngelmu* (having good knowledge) that is integrated with daily behavior. In spiritual or mystical form, the concept of understanding doesn't refer only to the intellectual side, but also the intuitive side. Such awareness is underlying Javanese behavior in all aspects of life, including social life and politics. Among the attitudes that have become the characteristics of Javanese life are *unggah-ungguh,* or how to interact with people based on time and place (*empan lan papan*); *kormat,* or respectful; and *tepo seliro,* or tolerant. At a glance, these manners seem feudalistic, but on a closer look, they also contain the influence of Islamic values, such as gratitude, respecting your parents, being humble, the teaching of simple life, a polite way of speech, and not associating others with God in worship (Soorah Luqman [31]: 12-19).

The definition of Javanese ethics is not based on rational consideration to determine something as "true" or "false", because the ethics of Java do not focus on *das sollen* (what aspired; what should be there later). As what Franz Magnis Suseno said in his book *The Ethnic of Java,* Javanese ethics are "ethical wisdom" rather than "ethical obligation".

This wisdom does not only deal with human relationships, but also how to treat animals and their environment (in Islamic terminology: *rahmatan lil 'alameen,* or a blessing for the entire universe). The concept of *Jumbuhing Kawula Gusti* (integration between people and government) or unity among commoners (*kawula*) and nobles (knights or kings) reflects the harmony between a ruler and the people. The two parties are interdependent. As a leader and protector, the ruler also needs adequate support from the people.

Even the ancient kings of Mataram (one of the biggest ancient kingdoms in Java), of them, would be sworn in front of a cannon in their inauguration as a symbol of a willingness to sacrifice their life to protect the people (*lamun siro madeg narapati*) and that the king would rather lose his life or dignity than violate the oath.

The relationship between Javanese people and nature is guided by a set of norms called *Sangkan Paraning Dumadi* as an effort to balance ourselves with nature that can only be obtained through the practice of *prihatin* (concern). *Sangkan Paraning Dumadi* is a concept of understanding the origin of the world and everything in it, and we can obtain this understanding only after we "conquer ourselves" by cleansing our hearts of lust and ego and living by the norms and ethics. The goal is often not physical or material gains, but rather to get perfection of knowledge and understanding of macro cosmos

71

and micro cosmos (*ngelmu kasampurnaan*).

This *Ngelmu Kasampurnaan* (to get perfection of knowledge and understanding of macro cosmos and micro cosmos) will bring the spirit of *Memayu Hayuning Bawana* or 'always active in developing harmonious life and saving nature.' A wise leader would not fail to implement *memayu hayuning bawana* which refers to environmental safety and sustainability. Pollution, environmental degradation, natural disaster, landslides, and drought are the results of humans greed, those who do not care about natural preservation and the future of mankind.

In politics, the purpose of the *memayu hayuning bawana* concept is to incite the spirit of the leaders in building a more peaceful world. This concept consists of: *memayu hayuning salira* (maintain the people's welfare), *memayu hayuning bangsa* (maintain national welfare), and *memayu hayuning bawana* (maintain the welfare of the world).

This concept should be the cornerstone of motion for leaders under the motto *Sabda Pandhita Ratu tan Kena wola woli* (a leader should be sincere and committed to what he says). This describes the character of a leader who leads fairly, with no partiality to high-rank groups or discrimination.

Consequently, it is reasonable that this set of ethical norms condemns leaders who fail to build peace or harmony in this world, including those who create war and disintegration, those who exploit natural resources for their benefit, and those who ruin justice for the sake of their cronies.

FROM JAVA TO THE WORLD

The modernization of the 20th century and the shift of Javanese life caused deterioration in the political authority of feudalistic rulers, but *Keraton* (Javanese palace) still exists as the preserver of the traditional Javanese culture and its spiritual teachings. However, the difference between *ningrat* (the aristocrats) and *kawula* (common people) becomes increasingly transparent, although this social stratification has lasted for so long that it is subconsciously embedded in the mind of the people. It is very hard to remove this social stratification in Java and its institutions because Javanese people are still holding on to the concept of *Jumbuhing Kawula Gusti*, the unity between people and the state, the unity among common people and aristocrats, as the reflection of harmony. That's why the *keraton still exists* in Central Java (Yogyakarta and Surakarta); they are needed as a symbol although time has changed.

The awareness among the leaders in Java that power or the throne is a tool to serve the people precedes the democratic system in Indonesia. The concept of *sugih tanpa banda, menang tanpa ngasorake, ngurug tanpa bala, digjaya tanpa aji* (being rich without possesions, winning without humiliating, attacking without troops, being powerful without magic) strongly depends on the government's determination to realize the people's prosperity. Another Javanese advice is *Saben wong glenggahi kelenggahanipun, mungguh, lungguh, sengguh*, meaning that everyone should be aware of their respective position. When the people are happy with a ruler's leadership, they will not protest or try to take over the throne, because they are aware that it is not their place and there is no reason to. Who becomes a king, should be a good king; who becomes a minister, should be a responsible minister; and those who are common people should be trustful people. Everyone should do their part completely for the common interest.

Social leader awareness and democratic leadership allow the people to channel their aspirations, so the old teaching of *nderek karsa dalem* (obey what the boss says) has essentially been abandoned. What applies now is a motto that says *ing ngarsa sung tulada, ing madya mangun karsa, tut wuri handayani* (provide a model; create a goal; and provide constructive support), which encourages the people to be *eling pracaya lan mituhu* (aware, trusting and obedient) to the leaders.

From there, emerged the spirit of cooperation, which came from the awareness that we cannot complete a work without the help of others. We will always need other people. This awareness then turned into the spirit of *bhineka tunggal ika* (unity in diversity) which should live in the heart of each Indonesian. It emphasizes that every person has a unique personality and that different abilities could complement one another.

Social norms that encourage people to live

guyup lan rukun (in harmony and peace), have mutual respect, and *gotong royong* (work together to solve problems) should be applied in daily life. Consequently, failure in living according to those norms will disrupt the harmony of social life, and thus, social sanction will be imposed on offenders.

The social dynamics of Javanese society are directed at the unity of every element to achieve collective goals. This harmony is not to be manifested only among fellow human beings (microcosmic) but also towards the nature (macrocosmic).

For a Javanese Sultan, his leadership is dedicated only to the people's happiness, as stated in the Javanese classic proverb: *kaprabon, kagem karaharjaning praja, kawula, tuwin lestarining budaya* (the throne is to build people's prosperity in social and cultural life). Therefore, a Sultan has to do constructive efforts in empowering the people and improving their life. His strong will comes from commitment and trust, to apply justice, and believe in the people's support. People always try to be good citizens. They have high hopes that their leader will improve their life and uphold justice for all. Conversely, the leader wants the people to support his programs. In line with the changes in society, this leadership characteristics will continue to change in meaning and implementation. This public is changing by the social needs and demands of each layer of the Javanese community.

Because this social awareness has subconsciously been embedded in the mind of Javanese people, the principles of *pracaya* (belief), justice, and dedication develop themselves to stay relevant with times. Conceptually, these efforts must be formulated precisely, as it determines behavior awareness. This behavior awareness will continue to exist and become social habits within the community if the leader can become a role model.

The magnificence of Javanese culture and universal values provide an exemplary attitude of leaders, such as *pramana* (living in justice without manipulation). Henri Bergson called it *elan vital force,* meaning the core of life and unity between a person and external elements. Another example is *pranawa* (open life, willingness to change and adapt), *prasaja* (simple life), *prasetya* (total devotion), and *prastawa* (caution).

In the end, such an exemplary attitude will lead the Javanese community to apply an egalitarian and democratic system through the *jumbuhing kawula gusti* concept. Between the leader and followers, there must be harmony; *mukti siji kabeh,* or if one dies, all die too. That's why tolerance becomes a Javanese measuring tool, where a single action done by one person will affect the whole community. And the nature of Javanese ethical wisdom guides the Javanese people to be *sepi ing pamrih rame ing gawe* (free of self-interest, always ready to work hard for society and the welfare of the world).

Although born in the womb of feudalism and mysticism (a mixture of Hindu mysticism and Islamic Sufism), Javanese leadership philosophy, especially *Hasta Brata,* substantially can be practiced by any leader of the modern democratic system because it can be a general guide for each potential leader to lead the people.

The philosophy of Hasta Brata may become Javanese culture's contribution to universal leadership values. Any leader willing to practice these values will undoubtedly make the people feel contented and become prosperous. No more lies or false promises because with *Hasta Brata*, people can select their future leader and set a moral standard for the candidates.

VI. From Java To The World

VII

CONCLUSION

The Javanese philosophy of leadership, especially Hasta Brata, has a very deep and universal meaning. Its teachings can be applied in every country as moral guidance in selecting future leaders.

Within this context, Hasta Brata is in line with and can even strengthen the modern democratic system to bring out truly qualified leaders that are needed by the people, instead of a leader groomed by the media, television, internet, and surveys.

Today we see so many leaders who pretend to be good and trustworthy during campaigns but turn out to be unreliable once they run the office, this is evidence of the absence of a leadership philosophy that should be held as a moral standard. Most elected leaders today are solely the result of a political pragmatism process to achieve the highest position in the country.

Even in Indonesia, the birthplace of this philosophy, leaders are elected solely because of a political process without regard to moral standards. Leaders are chosen merely because of concessions among political parties, and even if a leader is elected by the people directly, such a leader only appears good because of the role of mainstream media as well as unobjective surveys/pollings.

People should have a moral reference in electing their leader, and for that reason, Hasta Brata plays a critical role in society. Hasta Brata can use as a tool for the people to control their leader - if the leader deviates from the rules, then they have the absolute right to revoke the mandate they have given to him.

Hasta Brata serves as a sharp knife to the top (leaders) and protector to the people. Leaders who implement Hasta Brata in their leadership will be respected and remembered forever, and possibly be elected many more times. But if he does not, he will fall in disgrace and be condemned by the people.

At last, hopefully, this simple book can be a positive contribution to leadership values and provide benefits to anyone who reads it.

Thank You Very Much.

LEAVE YOUR REVIEW

If you enjoyed this book or found it useful I'd be very grateful if you'd post a short review on the website where you bought this book. Your support does make a difference and I read all the reviews personally so I can get your feedback and make this book even better.

Thanks again for your support!

OTHER BOOKS BY AUTHOR

These books are available on online marketplaces.

1) THE WISDOM OF JAVA

This book discusses the 12 principles of life rooted in moral, ethical, and philosophical principles that are still applicable in the modern era, specifically within the Javanese culture. There is a belief that if Javanese people successfully apply these 12 principles of life, they will achieve a life that is safe, peaceful, and harmonious, not only individually but also as a society.

Furthermore, these classical 12 principles of life can be applied in your daily life, regardless of where you are. The values contained within these principles are universal and can be practiced by anyone, anywhere, regardless of cultural or geographical differences. By practicing these 12 principles, you can attain personal harmony and peace, leading to a more meaningful life and moving away from excessive materialism.

Make "The Wisdom of Java" your motivational and spiritual book, guiding your personal development towards becoming a better human being.

2) THE WISDOM OF BALI

With its reputation as one of the most stunning and diverse tourist destinations in Asia, Bali attracts nearly 1,000,000 visitors from around the world each year. Geographically situated between the islands of Java and Lombok, Bali is one of over 17,000 islands that comprise the Indonesian Archipelago. It is famously known as the "Island of Gods" and has been featured in The Lonely Planet.

As the only island where the majority of its population practices Hinduism, Bali possesses a unique identity among the predominantly Muslim population of Indonesia. Hinduism is deeply rooted as the source of values, philosophy, and ethics for the Balinese people. It can be said that there is no single aspect of life in Bali that does not contain philosophical, spiritual, symbolic, or ethical meaning. This richness of culture, traditions, and religion is what makes Bali truly special.

This book can help you understand the symbolic meanings behind each tradition, ritual, and religious practice of the Balinese community. It can also serve as a travel guide before you visit Bali, ensuring that you respect the ethics, traditions, and regulations that are highly valued not only by the Balinese people but also by the entire Indonesian society.

This book can also be used as a motivational and spiritual book to heal your soul.

3) 31 DAILY ISLAMIC MOTIVATION FOR TEENAGERS

"31 Daily Islamic Motivation for Teenagers" is a powerful and uplifting book designed specifically for young minds seeking inspiration on their journey of faith. With 31 thoughtfully crafted passages, this book offers a daily dose of Islamic wisdom and practical guidance to empower teenagers. Each passage covers essential topics such as self-discovery, resilience, gratitude, and the importance of fostering a strong connection with Allah.

Through its concise and accessible format, this book encourages teenagers to incorporate Islamic teachings into their daily lives, fostering personal growth and a deeper understanding of their faith. It serves as a valuable companion, providing the tools and encouragement to navigate the challenges of adolescence with faith, courage, and compassion.

By instilling a sense of purpose and positivity, "31 Daily Islamic Motivation for Teenagers" empowers young readers to overcome obstacles, make informed decisions, and embrace their identities as proud Muslims. This book is an indispensable resource for any teenager seeking to strengthen their faith and navigate the complexities of teenage life with a resilient and spiritually enriched mindset.

ABOUT THE AUTHOR

Ahmad Dzikran is a freelance architect, web designer, and writer in Indonesia. He has written dozens of articles and several books in Indonesia on religions, politics, social life, and history. This title is his third ebooks published on the internet. Other titles are *The of Java*, *The Wisdom of Bali,* and *31 Daily Islamic Motivation For Teenagers.*

You can find more about him or his books by visiting Instagram @digibooks.info or contacting him his email: digitalbookschannel@gmail.com, or following his Instagram: @ahmaddzikran

Follow Ahmad Dzikran on Amazon Author Page.